FROM REALISM
TO REALITY
In Recent American Painting

FROM REALISM
TO REALITY

In Recent American Painting

VIRGIL BARKER

UNIVERSITY OF NEBRASKA PRESS

LINCOLN : 1959

*The inclusion of illustrations in this work
was made possible by a grant from the Woods
Charitable Fund, Inc. All paintings reproduced
are a part of the Frank M. Hall Collection,
University of Nebraska Art Galleries, unless
otherwise designated.*

Publishers on the Plains

UNP

TO

ALICE O'BRIEN

Prefatory Note

PLATFORM REMARKS ABOUT some slides, even if they happen to make a listenable lecture, become intolerable in print. A book is a written thing in which ideas must be linked in a smoother sequence and sentences must be given a different ring. Therefore the following pages would not in any case have been a literal transcript of what was spoken at the University of Nebraska in October of 1958.

Moreover, it seemed to everyone concerned with this book that the illustrations to document the discussion might well be not of the paintings used for the lecture-slides but, when possible, of paintings owned by the University of Nebraska Art Galleries. Accordingly, all but three of these reproductions are from such originals.

This has not in any way altered the ideas developed in the lectures, or even the order of their presentation; but it has necessitated considerable modification of expression in order to establish a genuine connection between the words and these pictures. I am grateful to the University of Nebraska for the opportunity to re-cast my material in this fashion because I am glad to join in thus directing attention to the importance of the University's still growing collection.

For the lectures in which mine constituted one event in a series, the prescription of the University Research Council is that the lecturers shall "from the backgrounds of their own specialties explore and interpret the implications of their knowledge for man and his place in the universe". A commentator on contemporary American painting is fortunate in that the painters themselves are concerned with that theme. They, along with practitioners of the other arts, along with theologians and philosophers and scientists, are deeply involved with the age. Not all of the painters feel obligated to be explicit in the content of their pictures, but from what they choose to paint and how they paint it their ideas may be inferred. For that reason my own ideas are merely incidental to theirs in this approach to "man and his place in the universe".

I nevertheless run the risk of frequently using the personal pronoun. For the true meaning of "I" is the limitation it puts upon the meaning of what is being said. I hope that will be the effect here because art criticism, as I conceive it, speaks neither for the painter nor to him. All I want to do is to speak for myself as part of the audience, and only to such others in the audience as may be interested. But the audience as a whole is the third factor in the total and continuing activity called art. The artist and his work come to little unless they attract others into participation. Among those others the critic happens to be articulate; he gives an account of his own experience so that others may in turn participate through agreement or disagreement—usually both at once.

VIRGIL BARKER

Contents

Illustrations

FROM REALISM
TO REALITY

in Recent American Painting

I

Painting Before the Armory Show

POPULAR REALISM:
  William Michael Harnett (1848-1892)

ACADEMIC IDEALISM:
  George DeForest Brush (1855-1941)

ACADEMIC REALISM:
  John Singer Sargent (1856-1925)

NATURALISM:
  George Wesley Bellows (1882-1925)

PAINTING IS ONE of the ways in which an age expresses its idea of what is real. Painters have not always used these words to describe what they thought they were doing, but that is one of the things they have always done. A

1

very notable characteristic of this twentieth century has been the way in which its adventurous-minded painters have sought to round out their instinctive responses to the age by some kind of philosophical attunement to the experience it offers; perhaps more than ever before in history, the painters themselves have been debating over the real, over what their art can say about it, over how to say it. This debate as carried on in the United States since the Armory Show in 1913 has indeed made these forty years (and more) into the experimental phase of the Cosmopolitan Period; but even in the preceding forty, the conservative phase of cosmopolitanism, certain anticipatory changes occurred that belong with the later ones to form a continuous though increasingly uneven development. What an earlier generation called realism has been succeeded by what the latest generation calls reality. Those two words have in common the core word "real", but in the craft and art of painting they designate qualities immensely far apart. The older pictures and the later ones have in common the medium of pigment, but they demonstrate the immensity of the change. Americans since 1880 have brought painting all the way from imitative imagery to total non-figuration, from an externally derived verisimilitude to an internally derived verity.

Between 1880 and 1915 four distinct but allied manners in painting were shiftingly prominent through the large exhibitions of the eastern cities. At the outset the *trompe-l'oeil* of William Michael Harnett was the widely popular form of realism despite the fact that the most influential painters, those who determined academic policies and awarded the prizes, considered it old-fashioned in technique and unrefined in subject. Before the new century opened, Harnett himself had been virtually forgotten, but minor examples of the kind by other hands were still exhibited on academic walls by privilege of membership. The idealism typified by George DeForest Brush appeared secure within the professional organizations, but whatever excitement could be worked up in regard to new pictures in the annual shows was largely centered upon the technicians of academic realism. This was a competent enough adaptation of French impressionism confined to "the more smiling aspects" of the world and its prosperous inhabitants, and was most brilliantly exemplified by John Singer Sargent. The Ashcan School, without themselves conquering the Academy, succeeded in extending subject-matter to include the seamier episodes of city life and thus made it possible for the young George Bellows to enliven the Academy's exhibitions with his flashing and soon flashy naturalism. Several hundred painters practicing these different procedures found it possible to tolerate one another and even one another's pictures because they agreed upon two things: that the reality with which the painter is properly concerned lies in nature and that the painter's proper business with that reality is to reproduce it as faithfully as he can. Their differences of practice were the consequence of differing ideas about which aspects of nature's reality are essential to the painted image.

The professed aim of *trompe-l'oeil* is visual illusionism, and any attempt that approaches success involves a degree of craftsmanship which must always command the admiration that is owed to the discipline of the difficult. The necessary conditions of carefully chosen subject material arranged under a managed illumination, of the fixed viewpoint and the directed eye—these all combine into the studio equivalent of a controlled experiment in the laboratory. Moreover, the intended result is in itself at least semi-scientific, an aim that has been present in occidental painting ever since the initiation of perspective and cast shadows about five hundred years ago. The whole procedure so strongly alters the normal way of seeing that the resulting image, though it be called optical realism, is actually a piece of mental idealism which happens to be partially verifiable in nature when it is subjected to the complicated artifice of preparation. This kind of painting maintains the perennial appeal of the tangible; in it sight is used as a particularly intense refinement of touch. At the very instant that the eye asks "Is this real?" the mind knows it is not. The popular success of such a picture consists in tempting the spectator to touch it, if only to confirm his negative knowledge that the image is not the object. Artistic qualities sometimes accompany this visual ventriloquism, but literal illusionism is artistically illusory.

The painters then coming back equipped with the latest European training inevitably rejected that popular realism—if only because its characteristic subject-matter, familiar things of use piled compactly on a study table or hung close together on a barn door, was so ordinary. Such painting was for them but one element in the tiresome provincialism of late-nineteenth-century America which they were vowed to eradicate. For their idealism involved much more than the studio practice; they were themselves idealists in their program for renewing the tradition of painting here. They organized themselves into the Society of American Artists and thereby so completely determined the cosmopolitan character of the period that in a single generation they took over the National Academy of Design itself. They maintained the studio conditions in which they worked as much like those of the laboratory as the illusionists had done, but in elevating their subject-matter from the triviality of *trompe-l'oeil* to the nobility of the figure, nude and draped, they also undertook to improve upon nature in accordance with a canon of beauty which they traced back to the great masters. They applied pigment with a freer brushstroke than was possible to the illusionist, but their results were sufficiently linear to be described as sculpturesque; the fixed pose and manipulated illumination also made their results another variety of still-life. Their canonical betterment of nature was of course a confessed idealism, but it was sometimes justified by the rather paradoxical claim that such idealism is art's way of making the reality of nature more real. This had at least one merit in remembering that there is such a thing as imagination in man, although the actual pictures these painters produced usually testified to the absence of that faculty in themselves.

Alongside this idealism there was a species of realism derived from French impressionism which was visually and technically livelier in spite of an ingrained academic discretion. Its practitioners often left the confinement of the studio in a search for fresher subjects and a fresher way of rendering them; they were still concerned with visual accuracy, but their interest shifted from the presumed permanence of exact detail to an over-all unity of momentary effect. This meant that the contrasting textures obligatory in *trompe-l'oeil* and prevalent in the sculpturesque figure gave way to a fairly uniform texture of pigment as the separate shapes of nature blurred or even disintegrated in the atmospheric shimmer; and this in turn pushed the spectator back from the painting itself to the painter's own chosen point of observation. All this exacted of the painter a very different but no less difficult kind of craft which, when mastered, rewarded him with a freedom of execution approaching spontaneity. Painterly brushwork became the means of (theoretically) registering everything at once—the drawn form and the coloristic intensity, together with the degree of light permeating the envelope of air. There still existed the implication that the supposed ocular accuracy was to be tested by direct comparison with nature, but the spread of increasingly fluent brushwork persuaded the eyes of most people into an easy acceptance of these pictures as self-sufficient. That was as it should be, for every successful painting, whatever its technical or visual idiom, makes eye and mind together content.

The differences between impressionist realism and impressionist naturalism are not superficial, perhaps, but they are plainly on the surface. The change that received the greatest censure at the time had to do with subject-matter—the ugliness of dirty streets and the vulgar intimacies of tenement interiors, garishly vivid people in drab clothes. Such things caused shudders of distaste in all who were too refined for their own good, and those among them who thought they could use the vocabulary of criticism complained much about the loss of subtlety and the lack of distinction in the coarser brushwork and the melodramatic exaggerations of this "dark" impressionism. Many sensitive souls were pained by the obviousness of everything, and they saw no compensation in the equally obvious gusto both for the life being depicted and for the pigment handled with a seemingly careless sweep to match the casualness of the subjects. In a time when subject-matter was important, this extension in its range was a good thing for the emotional needs of Americans in general; and in a time when technique was generally not inspiriting, this bravura could at least begin the demonstration that paint has an expressive character independent of any images it may record. Much of Bellows's popularity with a new mass public derived from a muscular flamboyance of execution which appears to triumph over more difficulties than are actually there.

The foregoing paragraphs do not give an adequate account of what happened between the formation of the Society of American Artists in 1876 and the opening of the Armory Show in 1913; they are merely the briefest possible description of how things were when American painters commenced The Great Change. Many of them, looking at the pictures in the Armory Show, recognized that realism of the eye, however it may be defined, does not constitute the reality of painting. This reality is brought into existence when the painter "realizes" (makes real, in the sense of Cézanne) an idea appropriate to pigment. Thus the art of painting began its twentieth-

century American adventure into what was then relatively unfamiliar territory. The key question was no longer:
How closely does the picture resemble appearances? The
question became: How effective is the picture's painterly
impact?

II

Naturalism in Painting
and Naturalism in Philosophy

THE LAYMAN, too, will have his own reasons for being dissatisfied with faithfulness to appearances as the painter's single obligation, or even his major one. My own reasons for that dissatisfaction with all forms of naturalism in painting derive naturally from the fact that whatever philosophy I can lay claim to is naturalistic. My philosophical ideas are out of William James, John Dewey, and George Santayana. To expound in fullness my personal corruption of that source material would certainly be a delaying action at the moment; I therefore offer in overly dogmatic form my justification of the foregoing paradox as being both logical and reasonable—those qualities are far from being identical.

Every kind of painting that exalts perception over conception to that degree reduces itself to spiritual superficiality. The naturalistic philosopher asks for an entire man in life, and in art for an entire experience—or the

9

nearest thing to entirety that the particular art can encompass. The complete man, the complete artist, the complete scientist—all want imagination at work because the human spirit is most completely itself when reaching for what is beyond. The imagination in art, as in science, finds that appearances are an incomplete account of reality. What is visible is caused by what is invisible; and the imagination, in both art and science, wants to penetrate to that. Paul Klee said: "Art does not render the visible; it renders visible." And a hundred years earlier William Blake told how he captured his visions: "I look through my eye, not with it."

This need for the exercise of the imagination is one of the reasons why art should be pushed to extremes. Doing that has a great deal more than therapeutic value. It has the spiritual value of discovery and recovery— which is my way of taking Aristotle's idea about art as "purgation". We live in swoops and spirals and pendulum-swings of thinking and feeling. It is art's business to give scope to all that by its own imaginative extensions of experience. "The excellence of every art is its intensity," said Keats. That is a very romantic assertion, but it applies equally well to the intensities of classic art. The participator in any art looks for its intensity in what is unique with it, and that is found in the qualities and possibilities that are inherent in the medium. In some such way the layman comes around to echoing the painter's question: How effective is the picture's painterly impact? The layman concludes that the painter's business is to develop the expressive character of paint because that is the art's medium of imaginative communication.

III

Pioneer Modernism

MAURICE BRAZIL PRENDERGAST
(1861-1924)

THE AMERICAN PAINTER of the Cosmopolitan Period who first found a permanently interesting way of answering that question was Maurice Prendergast. Only five years younger than Sargent, he worked in the climate of academism yet achieved his own freedom a quarter of a century before the larger liberation of the Armory Show. His personal style was not only prophetic of what was to come but also surpisingly complete in its own realization of the newly developing concept of painting. He did much more than open a road to the future; he got to the other side of a great divide between two territories of painting, and he did so with hardly a trace in his work of the toiling and sometimes tortured psychological journey recorded in the works of other pioneers of the

11

twentieth-century adventure. Prendergast's pictures are lyrics, with the charm of an unmaimed personality at ease in the art and enjoying the exercise of it. He may seem to have painted as a bird sings, but what he captured was the more difficult naturalness that lies only beyond knowledge and self-consciousness. He discovered the reality of pigment as a language different from all the other languages of art and he used it with a singularly pure intensity of visual sensation. This enables him immediately to dispense with the academic deference to appearances; he replaced that with a free calligraphy of the brush which was appropriately differentiated for watercolor and for oil.

His large-scale color-spotting in the aquarelles bears some resemblance to one manner of Paul Signac's, but the American's gay and captivating activity of design puts more than the Atlantic Ocean between him and the Frenchman, whose static shapes often approach inertness. Prendergast's watercolors not only appear but actually are spontaneous; but should anyone think them extemporized also, it then needs to be pointed out that only habitual foresight can keep repeating the air of happy accident. The proof of this with the pictures of Prendergast is that renewed looking so often yields something not previously perceived, particularly in nuance of color.

That last observation applies even more to his oils than to his watercolors, and it might be impossible to decide which group of pictures is the more important. When he moved from watercolor into oil the characteristic transparency was replaced by a no less characteristic impasto, the sparkle by a glow, and the attractive abruptness of

MAURICE PRENDERGAST: Neponset Bay. *Oil on canvas,*
4½″ x 32¼″.

stroke by a slower continuity of rhythm. The earlier jollity of mood was quieted by a thin film of wistfulness, and if compensation be needed for this change it can be found in the unfailingly sumptuous irridescence. *Neponset Bay* (preceding page) is an example of that phase of Prendergast's work which is best known to the general public through acquisition by widely distributed museums, and when these pictures are seen one by one in that scattered way each one seems reminiscent of the others. But if they are brought together in numbers an unexpected variety of effect results from otherwise unrealizable subtleties of color harmonies.

Neponset Bay is like many others by Prendergast in being named for a specific place, but none of the places can be discovered by visiting the geographical spot; they can be enjoyed only by the Prendergastian mental traveler. For this painter made the necessary break with the external world. The looking that he did with his eye was only preliminary and incidental; he emulated Blake and used his eye to look through. When he found in nature a scene that gave him delight, he then depicted no literal image of the scene but rather the delight itself. It is this which he put directly into coiling line and processional design, into every dragging or twirling brushstroke and every firm-handed pressure of the palette-knife.

Monumentalism was alien to his intent, for his note remains a blithe intimacy which is more rare than more imposing qualities in a time when sophistication taints the non-tragic personality with self-consciousness. To maintain a zestful gayety, even an exultant joy, into the twentieth century with the *élan* of a Matisse or the ardor of a Prendergast seems to require either astonishing good luck or even more astonishing self-knowledge. Perhaps the miracle of both these painters consisted in their combining both.

IV

The Influence of Cubism

STUART DAVIS

(1894-   )

THE BRAIN-WORK hidden within the charm of a Prendergast painting is not concealed as something shameful but
simply kept where it does not interfere with the effect.
The brain-work in a picture by Stuart Davis is featured
to the point of sometimes impairing the sensuousness the
eye desires.

Davis was born a generation later than Prendergast,
but he was started upon re-making his previously naturalistic vision by the same kind of pictures, those by the post-
impressionists. Very quickly, however, Davis pulled up a
generation further for the influence that defined the first
stage of his maturity, the influence from cubist pictures
and theory. He spent a now-famous winter in the self-
discipline of painting and re-painting an egg-beater nailed

15

to a studio table, varied with some accessories, of course, and these elaborate exercises taught him how to subject nature to two ways of thinking at once and how to combine the results at will.

He analyzed the object or the scene into a series of planes so as to choose those which could be most interestingly combined into a pictorial equivalent. He learned to use colors independently of those that might be present in nature, and thus to make the color relationships in his pictures a means of re-enforcing the interest of his reassembled planes. In this procedure Davis developed two other subordinate factors. One was the use of letters and even whole words to strengthen the planes or to function as planes in their own right. The other was the elimination of naturalistic textures in favor of a rather drily insistent uniformity of pigment texture, sometimes emphasized by the underlying grain of the canvas.

He had achieved easiness in this personal dialect when the good luck of a trip to Paris put a keener edge on the natural high spirits of his painting by a perceptive choice of expressive details and a witty juxtaposition of them in animated design. For many of us who were lucky enough to know Paris in the 'twenties, Davis's group of pictures to which *Arch Hotel* (page 17) belongs retain a great deal of the gayety permeating the city's complex imaginative effect. Davis preserves one important aspect that helped to make Paris a heaven on earth even for Americans who had no more intention than did Davis himself of dying in order to go on living there.

The wit thus manifested has been consistently shown also in Davis's other activities, one of which has been a

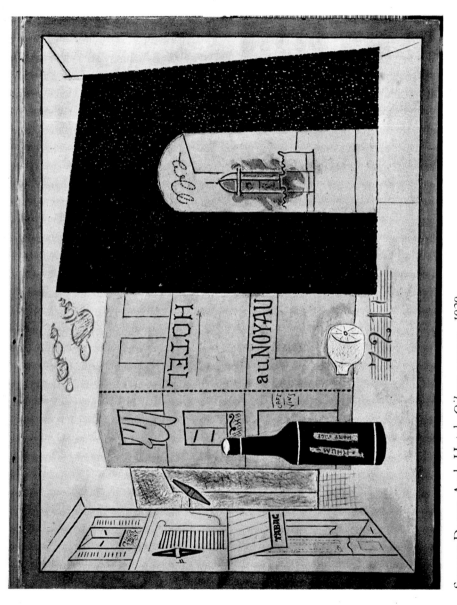

STUART DAVIS: Arch Hotel. *Oil on canvas, 1929,*
28¾″ x 39¼″ .

continuous verbal campaign on behalf of better thinking
about the experience of painting in general and about his
kind of painting in particular. He has talked and written
about the ends and means of art in a brilliantly paradoxical
way that has doubtless confused some but enlightened
many more. The prime paradox for many years was his
insistence that he was not at all the abstractionist the critics
immediately labeled him, but on the contrary a realist.
His claim was that the aspects of nature retained in his
paintings were, to begin with, chosen for their "reality",
which I interpret on more than one level of meaning.
Those chosen aspects possess a degree of actuality in being
recognizable; they so strongly concentrate the essence of
particular places that in the pictures they possess a sug-
gestiveness bordering on incantation; and they have a
special suitability to Davis's idea of pictorial activity.
The pictures did remain realistic to the extent that their
elements were individually recognizable, but that very
fact simply accentuated the arbitrary character of what
the painter was doing; they were from the first so clearly
headed toward abstraction that it is not surprising that
his large and vigorous decorations in recent years have
become entirely non-figurative.

This prevailingly aggressive intellectualism has had its
pitfalls, for no man can be as bright and as witty as Davis
without sometimes pushing his luck—in his case into
some strained verbalisms and some pictures of the forced
gayety which is dullness. It is this intellectualism, I think,
that prevents him from ever being spontaneous in the way
of Prendergast. Davis has sometimes not been light-
handed enough for his purposes, but he has rarely been

light-minded, and most of the time he has been success-
fully light-hearted. That, so far from being a trivial matter, is a major merit. To be intelligently entertaining is so
rare a talent in a painter that any member of the audience
can only show how seriously he takes it by trying to
match its lightness.

V

Early Romanticism

MAX WEBER
(1881-   )

JOHN MARIN
(1872-1953)

MAX WEBER AND John Marin, both belonging to the time
between Prendergast and Davis, present interesting con-
trasts not only with each other but also with the other
two—on the one hand with Prendergast's lack of self-
consciousness and with Davis's dramatization of it on
the other.

Weber was endowed with both curiosity and sensitivity
to such a degree that he responded to every important style
of the twentieth century in painting. His pictures accordingly changed their stylistic costume through the years,
but the knowingness of the changes had a kind of con-

21

sistency appropriate to the time. His most impressive early response in this way, before the personalized maturity of his middle years, was to both phases of cubism: with coloristic brightness in still-life to the analytic phase and with a darker-hued subtlety in the figure to the synthetic phase. In *The Forest* (page 23), executed midway through his painting career, he exploits the richness of pigment in what strikes me as a somewhat Cézanne-like way. This picture shares the mood of gravity pervading his impressive figure-pieces of about the same time—those slow-gesturing nudes so perceptively described by someone as "Assyrian" because of the orientalized strength and weight which make the handling of the pigment more voluptuous than the women themselves. That pigment quality seems no less strong in this landscape, and it thereby manifests the deep emotionalism which has all along been Weber's most fortunate as well as his most tragic trait.

The considered and deliberate pace of Weber's mind and art is in striking contrast to Marin's seemingly swift but no less considered perception and execution. (This is a description of a difference, with no implication that either is intrinsically superior to the other.) Part of this is properly due to the fact that Weber worked in oil and Marin in watercolor; yet Marin, with much effort in his later career, succeeded in making oil yield him a matching animation. However, his importance in American painting derives from his watercolors which, in several manners through the years, were consistently directed toward achieving the visually dynamic impact which for him was always the major significance of the whole world of sense experience.

MAX WEBER: The Forest. *Oil on canvas, 1931, 30″ x 40″.*

JOHN MARIN: Pertaining to Nassau Street, New York.
Watercolor on paper, 1936, 25⅜″ x 20¼″. Bequest of
Frances Sheldon, University of Nebraska Art Galleries.

Pertaining to Nassau Street, New York (page 25) is an example of a manner which to me seems less successful than his broader washes of the brush and dashings of intenser color across the paper. In this manner a masterpiece like *Lower Manhattan* (Museum of Modern Art, New York), by means of a distortion of extraordinary intensity even for Marin, conveys the entire range of city sensations—sudden heights, pressuring speeds, shattering noises—through the single sense of sight. Other pictures of other scenes by Marin can often make me catch my breath, but he himself never seems to be breathless. His way of making a painting is one of the superlative combinations, about half and half, of the optical and the mental. He made himself the master of the momentary sweep of the eye that is identical with the sweep of imaginative comprehension. Mind and sight together energize the scene; hand and brush together convey the energy. His stenography of sight sensations constructs the picture in tensions that are, after all, directed and reconciled into that equilibrium which he so often called "blessèd".

VI

A New Classicism

CHARLES SHEELER
(1883-   )

GEORGIA O'KEEFFE
(1887-   )

MARIN'S EQUILIBRISTIC dance across the tight-wire of visual changeableness is the opposite of Charles Sheeler's visualization of changelessness. Some early exercises in semi-abstraction under a discipline of cubism quite as thorough-going and as intelligently done as that by Stuart Davis were the means by which Sheeler extricated himself from the naturalistic fluency of his teacher, William M. Chase. With a vision thus freshened, Sheeler then advanced to a new kind of realism; by fastidious omission of detail and tightening of shapes he often achieved the effect of essen-tializing a structure till then concealed below the surface

28

CHARLES SHEELER: Barn Reds. *Tempera on cardboard,* *1938,* 10⅜" x 12⅞".

of a scene. It was as if he were brushing away some film in nature to reveal a semi-Platonic ideal reality actually there but previously unrecognized through taking the ordinary for granted. In this manner all his subjects are "taken from life", and in the successful pictures they are taken quite a long way. Many times he reaches the verge of abstraction itself even in images which may seem semi-photographic to the casual eye. But every sign of motion, every hint of wandering air, every trace of dust, every possibility of sound—all such indications of ordinary experience of actual things have vanished in a deep-freeze of immaculate immobility.

Despite the difference of Sheeler's pictures from those of Marin and Davis, his compositional procedure is essentially the same as theirs: the analysis of a scene into a series of planes followed by a readjustment of them into a pictorial equivalent. Sheeler's readjustments are relatively slight in themselves, so that they often escape notice, but they are there. Consider one or two in *Barn Reds* (page 29), for instance. Note the escape from deadness in the lower right area through the slight shifts in the diagonal lines as the intervening fence post makes them disappear and reappear. Note also the arbitrary treatment of the small shadows that fall on the slanting wall at the lower left; Sheeler wants those particular shapes right where they are, but in naturalistic terms they imply a shift in the angle of the strongest light in the picture. Such departures from naturalistic exactness are not flaws, but on the contrary pictorial gains; together with the abstract quality of the illumination itself, they are essential to the strangeness extracted from or imposed upon the familiar. And in this picture all such details are rightly of little importance compared to its most effective feature: the sensation of largeness caught in so small a picture. In a time that craves bigness in a literal way and a lot of excitement with which to fill it, a small painting which expands in the remembering mind becomes important for that very reason.

In her early work Georgia O'Keeffe sometimes painted exorbitantly enlarged flowers to startle the eye with a semi-human individuality in non-human things; in these and later pictures precision of drawing and subtle loveliness of texture earned a wondering admiration. In *New York, Night* (page 33), O'Keeffe chose the problem of retaining immensity while working on almost the scale of intimacy. She has been so successful that within a canvas height of only a little more than three feet she has caught the visual incredibility of the towers that make deep and narrow ravines of the streets so far below. The warm colors of man's contradiction of the night here embody a cold vision of height.

With both Sheeler and O'Keeffe the needle of the mind oscillates within a seemingly narrow range and stays very near the point of equipoise. Both seek a spiritual permanence in visual form—Sheeler by an ascetic omission of the accidental, resulting usually in clear-lighted austerity; O'Keeffe by an active transcendence of the actual, resulting often in exultancy. In both there is the recurrence of mankind's old longing for something steady beyond change, something permanent beyond the temporary.

Both Sheeler and O'Keeffe paint man-made things, a whole man-made environment, but from it man himself is

GEORGIA O'KEEFFE: New York, Night. *Oil on canvas,*
1929, 40⅛″ x 19⅛″. Collection of the Nebraska Art Association, University of Nebraska Art Galleries.

physically absent. That very absence dramatizes the fact of man's existence, for these empty places are waiting for man to come back. The reason for his absence, as I interpret it, is that the classic vision minimizes the individual to the vanishing point. Classicism aspires to impersonality, universality, which is not necessarily inhuman but is certainly supra-personal. From that universal the separate creature is excluded, and the consuming ego in which most people permanently live is at least temporarily transcended.

That is why most people find it difficult to respond to the classic temper in any art. In painting they remain indifferent to what they think is lack of feeling. But for those who can experience the impersonality of classic art even temporarily, what a relief it affords! from the trivialities of oneself as well as of other people. Both Sheeler and O'Keeffe can "realize" that state of serenity, can make that exceptional state of mind a reality of visual sensation, for however short a time.

In many of their pictures, in fact, this classicism becomes so intense that it radiates something like the romanticism of the strange. And this suggests something further that applies, I think, to the whole history of art. Classicism of spirit, whenever and wherever it occurs, in Greece or China or India or the United States, is the most romantic development of all in man's art. For the record of man, as far back as records exist, show him passionately wrong, wilfully ignorant, knowingly cruel, and incurably lazy. Yet only man in all the universe, so far as he can know, makes art as his dream of perfection, as his way of completing what is otherwise an incomplete experience.

VII

Later Romanticism

MARSDEN HARTLEY
(1877-1943)

YASUO KUNIYOSHI
(1893-1953)

ALTHOUGH CLASSICISM may be a romantic event in art history, its pictorial results do not manifest the irregular break-outs of romanticism. A picture by Sheeler or O'Keeffe secures much of its effect through emphasizing the factor of conscious control to the point of inducing the spectator to think that everything has been foreseen from the beginning. One of the marks of romanticism is often supposed to be an equally unmistakable effect of happy accident. But, as I remarked in commenting on Prendergast, that of itself requires pictorial foresight in the painter.

It is easier to credit foresight of this kind to Marsden

Yasuo Kuniyoshi: Room 110. *Oil on canvas, 1944,*
44″ x 34″.

Marsden Hartley: Mt. Katahdin, Autumn, No. 1. *Oil on canvas, 1939-40, 30″ x 40″.*

Hartley than to most romantics because his designs are themselves slow-moving, even as his conversation was, even as in life he developed slowly through several phases before reaching the authoritative utterance of his later years. But Yasuo Kuniyoshi's mind operated with greater rapidity as well as greater subtlety; his temperament indeed seemed to me like quicksilver in its elusiveness and its variable mingling of qualities, some oriental and some occidental. His work as a whole, therefore, remains unseizable in a single adjective; but Hartley's work, through all of its changes as influenced by other painters, was on the way to grandeur.

His painting at the Nebraska gallery, *Mt. Katahdin, Autumn, No. 1* (opposite page), is among the most impressive of the late pictures in which he attained his fulfilment. Everything has been consistently translated into the language of paint. Naturalistic textures were probably the first thing to go; in their place is a frank reliance on the texture of pigment throughout. There is no slightest hint of naturalistic motion in the separate shapes; instead, the design itself moves, mounting in steps, heaving up into the limited release of the sky with a linear rhythm that is calming even in its topmost jaggedness. Naturalistic space is ignored for an equivalent constructed by color relationships in which the lower-center warmth actually strengthens the over-all effect of cold remoteness akin to the ice-blue strangeness of the painter's own eyes.

Kuniyoshi's *Room 110* (page 37), though painted during the Second World War, has none of the high-keyed pain and anger in the slightly later pictures directly affected by the war; this one has the delicate strength of construction and the reticent colorism which marked the middle phase of his development. It also retains much of an earlier puckishness, an engagingly sly pleasure in giving a surprise, which was more obvious in earlier work; here it is subtilized by tenderness. Too positive to be called winsome, too gay to be called wistful, this picture is an indescribable blend whose only adequate identification is the painter's own name.

Most romantics, whether artists or merely people, evolve into the permanently tragic mood. Life almost never answers to all the demands that the romantic makes upon it, and neither does art. A soft-tempered romantic subsides into a sad resignation which has too large a streak of self-consoling pleasure in it to be quite convincing; and there is a lot of this to be found in contemporary American painting, visualized as languid or theatrical soft-focus nostalgia. The innately strong romantic, such as Hartley, can conquer the tragedy by acceptance. I do not detect that finality in the tragic coloring of Kuniyoshi's last paintings, but in the picture at Nebraska he sings an elegiac lyric about the pathos of memory-haunted trash.

VIII

Romantic Realism

REGINALD MARSH
(1895-1954)

EDWARD HOPPER
(1882-   )

REGINALD MARSH AND Edward Hopper, like Kuniyoshi, cannot be labeled without the injustice of ignoring factors in their art other than the one singled out by the label. Both are clearly romantic—Marsh in a highly extrovert fashion, Hopper as clearly in an introverted way. But their romanticism itself depends upon a degree of realism to make it as effective as it is. Thus it may appear that both give life and nature a larger credit for their pictures than the painters already discussed.

Both Marsh and Hopper are conscious of pigment, but they do not give it the importance that the others do.

41

They seem to concentrate upon images which, alongside those of the preceding modernists, are realistic almost to the point of naturalism. But they do not actually represent in the older academic sense; rather, they re-present.

For they do not work direct from nature. Marsh made multitudes of quick sketches at every opportunity, but they were practice to keep his eye and hand in training. Hopper does not work in the presence of nature at all. Marsh with his sketches, Hopper without them, compose their pictures in their heads and execute them in their studios. For both the shaping process is the memory—rapid with Marsh, slow with Hopper. Memory as a way of achieving design has this supreme virtue: that the realism it produces is permeated with imagination. Memory's filter excludes the unimportant, the inessential; what remains is significant both pictorially and emotionally—and pictorially significant because the picture has actually been shaped by the emotion which determined the memory all along. Both men work from the basis of a multitude of perceptions, but out of that multitude the significant ones are ordered by a concept. The concept is the mood, the details are out of what was seen; the memory therewith creates images which could conceivably happen in nature but actually happen only in the painters' minds. If the resulting pictures seem to have been handed to the painters pre-designed by nature, that is merely the evidence of their skill in fulfilling their own intentions.

Marsh manifested several moods through his work, but they all unite on one theme—the life of the city crowd. He had no interest in non-human nature, the landscape; he was not interested even in man-made surroundings, the

REGINALD MARSH: The Park Bench. *Tempera on panel, 1933, 24″ x 36″.* Collection of the Nebraska Art Association, University of Nebraska Art Galleries.

EDWARD HOPPER: Room in New York. *Oil on canvas, 1932, 29" x 36".*

city-scape, except insofar as they helped to display people. Nor was he much interested in people as individuals. *The Park Bench* (page 43), and some others by him in the depression 'thirties came nearest to endowing his people with some measure of personality, but even so the figures have a greater significance as types. Well before the depression was over, Marsh erupted with his natural buoyancy into designs wherein people become creatures surging and swaying and revolving in dizzying masses of anonymous energy. Sand lizards in tight bathing trunks, shopping crowds, burlesque audiences, whirling skaters, and delirious riders on merry-go-rounds—the creatures that make up such human hives may be separately repulsive or frightening; but Marsh's pictures manifest an undefeatable relish for the vast swarming of that mass life.

Marsh gives many variations of mood on one theme, and Hopper gives a greater variety of subjects—landscapes, city-scapes, city interiors, all of them with figures and without; but they all reiterate the single mood of aloneness. This does not always involve loneliness as something of which the people in the pictures are themselves aware; for that may or may not be the case. But every person and every object in a Hopper painting exists in separation from everything else. *Room in New York* (opposite page) is shown from the outside looking in; the people inside are so separate from the spectator that they are unaware of him. The man and the woman are also separate from each other. It is the light that makes the essential pictorial impact. In fact, light makes the mood of every successful Hopper painting, whether it is the somber glare of a movie-house lobby or the soaring shine above a Cape Cod lighthouse. In the Nebraska picture the light divides man and woman from each other, even as it divides the two of them from us looking on. This double image of aloneness gives me a feeling that the painter himself is lonely. Yet to know loneliness and also to know that someone else knows it is to mitigate it into a kind of communion.

IX

A Different Climate of Painting

THE NINE painters just discussed, with Prendergast added as an elder herald of the new dispensation, are representative of American painting for the quarter of a century following the Armory Show. Their ideas and procedures collectively produced a solid body of work occupying a position definitely in advance of that of the generation immediately preceding and constituted a permanent gain for the art of painting in the United States. They all experienced the opposition and even misrepresentation which experimental artists have been subjected to since 1800, but their work now presents no serious difficulty of comprehension to anyone accustomed to art museums and exhibitions. Their work is indeed so widely accepted that it is not incongruous to take a look at it through a set of three ideas advanced by John Steuart Curry in his thinking about art in this country—ideas which could not survive as part of the new climate of painting during the last two decades.

The first idea is that art belongs in the realm of everyday life. Some kind of art does belong in the daily life of everyone, right enough. That is like saying that religion should be practiced on week-days as well as on Sundays. Everybody will agree, and practically everyone will then point out that the others don't do it. The real difficulty with this truism about art is that those who preach it as a truth tend to preach further that the art for everyday living should also deal only with everyday subjects. No: whatever art gets into the daily life of anybody may deal with anything. And perhaps its presence there would be the very reason why it should deal with anything and everything that is not familiar in "real life".

Curry's second idea is harmonious with his first: that art should be comprehensible. In conjunction with the first, it is plain enough that he thought art should be understandable by everybody. Not necessarily. Are science and religion and philosophy thus commonly understandable? And is art any less complex, any more simple, than they? Therefore this idea of Curry's needs the cautioning word: Distinguish. Comprehensible to whom? An art conditioned to the understanding of everybody, or even the majority under modern conditions of a mass public, would be undesirable as well as unfeasible. There are many publics, and to each its own art. For theoretically the member of any public can shift to any other public; and unless that cultural mobility is maintained by the lure of art that needs effort to be understood, what chance is left for mental growth and, among other things, social self-betterment?

Curry's third idea is also entirely consistent with the other two, but much of the painting produced in the last two decades makes it seem the most out-of-date among the three. This idea is that art should be motivated by genuine love and affection. Of course a great deal depends upon the strength of such emotions, and even more upon the quality of the mind that feels them. No doubt that state of mind can produce likable art, but motives morally less admirable or perhaps even reprehensible have a way of making art more intense and interesting in human terms. It seems both factually more accurate and psychologically more truthful to say that any motive is valid if art results, art being provisionally described at this point as the clarification or the intensification of experience.

As things have turned out, an adventurous younger generation, arbitrarily defined as the painters born since 1900, have found Curry's program inadequate, or would have if they ever heard of it. The 'forties and the 'fifties have been spiritually more difficult than the 'twenties, more so than even the 'thirties in some ways. The general debate about art itself has sharpened, and painters especially have become involved in re-thinking the problems of the interactions between life and art, of the language of painting, of just what can be expressed in that language—in short, the all-inclusive problem of reality and what aspects of reality belong to the art of painting. For the nature of reality is that every generation with an experience of its own has in consequence its own idea about the real. Moreover, reality lies within the other domains of religion and philosophy and science as well as in the domain of the arts; and in all of them the search for the real must be made. In all of them no motive less ambitious could either make them worth doing or account for what has already been done.

X

Imagination, Fanciful and Realistic

MORRIS GRAVES
(1910-   )

ANDREW WYETH
(1917-   )

A GOOD PICTURE BY Andrew Wyeth and a good one by
Morris Graves become more interesting in each other's
company because both surprise the mind with strangeness.
Their contrasting techniques of Wyeth's hyper-precision
in seemingly objective rendering and Graves's sometimes
baffling calligraphic suggestion derive from radically
different ways of thinking, but they both result in fantasy.

Graves seeks his reality in the far yonder, on wings of
Zen. This form of mysticism, like all others, affirms the

51

unreality of what is apparent to the senses, so that all images animated by it are committed to the paradox of using what it considers to be the illusory perceptions of sight to suggest what cannot be seen. Less mystical natures who can get along without symbolism in painting may still welcome the imaginativeness in a successful example because it at least partially domesticates the otherwise unknown; for such minds, the non-realism of the intensely imagined can be a visual experience needing no symbolism to make it more real.

In one group of pictures strongly influenced by Mark Tobey's device of "white writing" and usually having the word "moonlight" in their titles, Graves has depicted some birds not of the natural world, each one of which is misted in a solitude that will never be broken. The sense of separation that Hopper's pictures convey is between man and man; Graves's bird-personified loneliness is that of being lost in a universe. Another group of pictures using both birds and fish have in their titles some reference to "outer" or "inner" or "higher" space; these are not completely self-contained in design, but have direction lines diagonaling outward without return. And a third group, to which belong the *Eagle of the Inner Eye* (page 53) and a few others with titles that refer either to the inner eye or to being "in the rock", show creatures in hiding and usually threatening all who would break in upon their creature remoteness. These are generally contained within slightly irregular but tight oblongs with slanting ends; this shape and the distortion of the figure together make a leftward thrust, sometimes with strength. For all of Graves's intention to symbolize, therefore, his

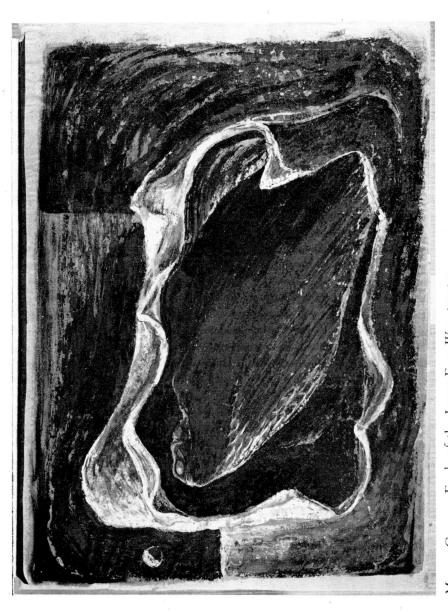

Morris Graves: Eagle of the Inner Eye. *Wax tempera on paper, 1941, 19¼″ x 26½″*.

ANDREW WYETH: Spring Beauty. *Water color on card-board, 1943, 20" x 30".*

strictly pictorial qualities are communicative in their own right.

Such meanings cannot always be verbally clarified; and I think it is relatively unimportant that they should be, though it is always interesting to try. The reality of these unrealities may often be obscure, but it lingers. Since Graves's thought is oriented to an oriental form of mysticism, I suppose he is hoping to escape from the self by the inner door of the imagination. He may be hoping to get beyond the world of the senses into undifferentiated being; he may be engaged in that quest so magnificently described as "the flight of the Alone to the Alone". I do not have to share in such desires in order to find many of these images lovely, even alluring in their muted way. Some years ago a young woman whose name I never learned said before one of Graves's pictures: "It keeps whispering of moonlight." Is not that enough?

One general qualification I would make has to do with what I think is still a rather self-conscious adoption of an attitude. Contemporary experience is thus impaired for a great many people, and usually most impaired for those most concerned with how this experience is different from that of other times. The relatively few public statements made by Graves have, I think, more than a trace of this; and for me it is the probable explanation of his failure so far to achieve the highest level of imaginative creation. He has not yet pushed through a cultivated mysteriousness to the deeper mystery that lies beyond.

Wyeth, too, wants to escape from self. "When I paint I try to obliterate Andy Wyeth." Impossible as it is to do that in creating art, it often gives nobility to the result;

it does so with Wyeth as it did with Mondrian. As Graves turns inward, so Wyeth tries the outer door of a devoted examination of nature; and his amazing craft, registering perceptions that seem minutely exact, almost always gives the surprise of more than was known to be there. In spite of the uncountable meticulous details, that "more" is not primarily factual; it is a unifying vision determined by an all-pervasive foreboding, ranging from simple pathos to obscure dread. The technical means of this unification is the management of the illumination, which is not always the light, giving a pictorial reality more intense than ocular realism. Wyeth has written about the tree in *Spring Beauty* (page 55) as actually existing on his home place since his childhood, and that is one of the reasons why no one else looking at it in nature would see what he has seen. In minds of this quality, the very longing for impersonal perfection in the work produces the most subtly personal accent of all. "Character teaches above our wills," wrote Emerson. In the genuine artist, temperament speaks over the conscious intent; it colors the outer world with the dye of inner vision.

XI

The Painting of Ideas

RICO LEBRUN
(1900-   )

JACK LEVINE
(1915-   )

PETER BLUME
(1906-   )

GRAVES AND WYETH ARE using pictures to contain ideas that are not inherent in paint. Wyeth, aiming to let nature speak for itself, is fulfilling his own idea about nature; and though it is presented in as objective a way as he can manage, it nevertheless constitutes an interpretation. Graves is of course quite conscious that he interprets, but what he tries to say that is specifically Zen or even more generally mystical requires, I think, some kind of

59

initiation from outside of painting. Three other painters
may be grouped together, in contrast to most of the others
being discussed on this occasion, for the elaboration and
the power of the non-pictorial thought which they put
into their major works.

That of Rico Lebrun is traditionally religious, but his
presentation of it is far from being traditionally academic. This creates difficulties for a great many people
among the churchly audience, but not for the audience
aware of recent painting. Jack Levine's larger pictures
are a much more mature continuation of the social consciousness which was the dominant theme through the
depression decade. Peter Blume concerns himself with
ambitious philosophical and allegorical visualizings of
the state and fate of civilization. This varied content is
not necessarily un-pictorial, and with these three it never
becomes definitely anti-pictorial; but because it is non-
pictorial in character the artistic results vary much in
quality. These three are among the most explicit painters
today in painting ideas about "man and his place in the
universe". Therefore, despite their marked dissimilarities
in technique, they afford an opportunity to think a little
about their kind of thinking and its relation to the art
of painting.

At this point I must insert a personal opinion which
affects my reactions to idea-paintings in general, in this
or any other time. I'm all for thinking—about everything;
and by everybody who wants to do it—even painters. The
kind of thinking I am describing now, in its appearance
with these three painters, not only arises in life as a part
of living but also remains a vital part of life in affecting

Rico Lebrun: Woman of the Crucifixion. *Duco on masonite,* 8' x 4'.

JACK LEVINE: Pensionnaire. *Oil on masonite, 1945,* 36″ x 28″.

belief and action. At one time or another it becomes the content of every art, according to circumstances and the temperament of the individual artist; but in the history of every art it is something that comes and goes. With the painting of the further past I have found it always desirable to get an intellectual comprehension of such content in order to understand the part that painting has played in history, but it is beside the point for what I value most: the direct response to color, drawing, composition, handling—the use of the medium for embodying the painter's own response to the world.

I don't presume to say that any man or any painter should be different from what he is in order to suit my taste, and explicit ideas and feelings about "man and his place in the universe" are necessary to some painters in order that they shall paint at all. Moreover, they do honor to anyone who cares for them passionately and good to anyone else who can share them. For myself, I like best to find such ideas where I think they are best suited: in religious scriptures, in philosophic books, in scientific investigations, in political or economic programs—and all of these activities have their own kind of art in the presentation of their own material. When I meet with them in painting, my interest in them begins to evaporate as soon as I have examined them. This is why I find the Nebraska-owned pictures by the three men whom I group together at this point rather more interesting than most of their ambitious pictorial pronouncements about "man and his place in the universe".

Lebrun's *Woman of the Crucifixion* (page 61) is presumably one of the many pictures and studies made in the course of the lengthy development of his well-known triptych of *The Crucifixion,* recently installed at Syracuse University. My admiration for this Nebraska picture starts with the fact that it (quite literally) stands on its own feet as an independent creation. This woman of breathing stone, draped in something that is both cloak and armor, her face fixed in the stare of fatalistic agony, watches something that we do not see; it might be Warsaw or Hiroshima. What my words describe is the image; what I experience before the painting is from the expanding force of the spiky distortions and the night-flare lights and darks.

Levine's *Pensionnaire* (page 63) is different from several of his more ambitious efforts in a way that seems fortunate to me; it is more concentrated in design, not impaired by competing areas of visual interest, and it does not suffer from the forcing of satire which occasionally appears in his kind of "social comment". The humanly emotional element here is simple compassion; the El Greco type of fiery power is here translated into pathetic ineffectualness. Still here is the spirited assurance of brushwork that is the hallmark of Levine the painting phenomenon, although the size of the canvas does not give him as much scope as the larger ones for that flamboyant flicker of dancing whites which has so often been an almost dissociated counterpoint across the often ominously dark but always substantial figures.

Blume's *White Factory* (page 67) is a pellucid continuation of the "immaculate" tradition—through the rapid changes of the twentieth century the continuation of any style for only a decade is enough to constitute a

Peter Blume: The White Factory. *Oil on canvas, 1928,* 20" x 30". Collection of the Nebraska Art Association, University of Nebraska Art Galleries.

"tradition". Not only does Blume analyze the planes and clarify them in juxtaposition; he also retains the characteristic clearness of color. In his large-scale philosophies in paint Blume's color sense is often bizarre and produces clashes which are doubtless intentional; and they all carry a burden of detailed allegory which does not complicate the effect of this smaller picture in which the painting itself is no less thoughtful.

XII

An Imagery of Ultimates

HYMAN BLOOM
(1913-)

IVAN LeLORRAINE ALBRIGHT
(1897-)

AFTER WHAT I HAVE just said about non-pictorial ideas in paint, probably some will think me inconsistent in what I want to say about the work of Hyman Bloom and Ivan Albright. Emersonian scripture on this point is well known. "A foolish consistency is the hobgoblin of little minds. . . . With consistency a great soul has simply nothing to do." Anyone who accepts a naturalistic philosophy should certainly get rid of hobgoblins; therefore that first sentence gives me courage. From any implication of egotism in quoting the second sentence I can free myself

70

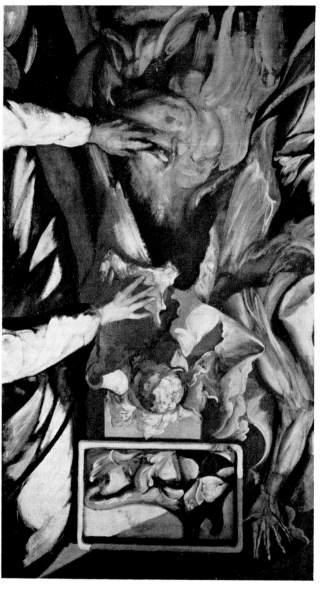

HYMAN BLOOM: The Anatomist. *Oil on canvas, 1953.*
70½″ x 40½″. Courtesy of the Whitney Museum of American Art, New York.

Ivan LeLorraine Albright: Fleeting Time Thou Hast
Left Me Old. *Oil on canvas, 1929-30, 20¼″ x 30¼″.*
Courtesy of the Metropolitan Museum of Art, George A.
Hearn Fund, 1950.

by claiming that I shall presently demonstrate I am consistent, and therefore no "great soul". But if, after read-
ing, anyone still thinks I am not consistent I can fall back
upon Zero Mostel, on the radio before the days of tele-
vision, with his chant of "I said yes—I said no—flexible
mind!" Or I can change to Whitman: "Very well, then,
I contradict myself." But in quoting him I should not
like for anyone to think that I think those words are
poetry.

Bloom and Albright are not represented at Nebraska,
but I include them here because I think that they are
major painters among those of the present time and that
they are saying important things with the accent of our
time's experience. Their themes are as old as the experience of man—the themes of decay and death—so that their
contemporary accent simply re-affirms the continuity of
human life and art. In medieval Europe these themes were
a part of daily life, as Curry thought art should be; they
are still universals of experience and should therefore be
acceptable in familiar art today. But their fatedness and
their grandeur require an intensity of artistic realization
which rarely occurs; the fact that Bloom and Albright
match the medieval intensity with a startling immediacy
of vision catches many people unprepared, and some of
them take refuge in what they think is righteous indigna-
tion in retaliation for being so profoundly disturbed.

From the first, Bloom has been a colorist, impasting
jewel-rich pigment in synagogue splendors and loaded
chandeliers of light. Through a semi-abstract phase of
ambiguous images he passed to a melodrama of death,
saying "Death is charged with energy. It is a fruitful area

of one's emotional life." In his pictures of dismembered corpses he faces up to death, and so faces it down. The riders in the fresco of the Campo Santo at Pisa hold their noses at the rotting corpses which they pass on the road, but the fact of death is not a direct experience for the spectator of the picture. Bloom rejects the intermediary gesture and asks us to look directly at the refuse that once was human. In New England he might be remembering many lines of poetry by New England's Emily Dickinson, who also, but with a quieter eloquence, learned to live with the fact of death. Bloom enlarges the look of it from a single still-human countenance to bodies whose humanity has been violated on the dissecting-table, as in *The Anatomist* (Whitney Museum of American Art, New York) (page 71). No human personality can be discerned in these raw animal remains; they are on the way to becoming part of the universal garbage into which all living matter ultimately deliquesces. There lies the shock, for the visual is more naked than the verbal.

Albright has described one of his principal earlier themes in words: "Women whose torrid flesh resembled corrugated mush". He also paints men—men sufficiently decayed to show that Albright is impartial as between the sexes. He has no hatred or even dislike that I can see for any person as an individual; all his figure-pieces, and the still-lifes as well, are elegies on the theme of *Fleeting Time Thou Hast Left Me Old* (Metropolitan Museum of Art, New York) (page 73). The fascination of these pictures derives in part from the fact that the painter's intense emotion seems buried so deep below the surface of his litany of the doom of being a human being. Whatever is strong for a time corrupts into its opposite, and the nightmare of decay can be as splendidly irridescent as health. Along with the spectral artifice of the illumination devised by Albright, the spectator's eye crawls slowly over the picture surface; the masquerade of an arbitrary optical realism reveals a truly pictorial reality of the identity of life and death.

Bloom sees an anonymous livingness in the inanimate discards that once were human; Albright sees pullulating life in all things animate and inanimate. The vision of both is too powerful to be condemned as morbid except by the timidly genteel. It is the power that makes people want to refuse the experience. But until decay is accepted as also an engrossing spectacle, the real significance of growth remains unrealized; and until death is known in its full reality, bestial as well as spiritual, life itself cannot be fully savored. These two painters come to terms with mortality; the authority of their painting validates the violence of their vision.

XIII

Action-Painting

HANS HOFMANN
(1880-)

THEODOROS STAMOS
(1922-)

ONE THING ABOUT BLOOM and Albright together that seems wonderful to me is the completeness with which they have accepted the consequences of their own ideas; they have painted dangerously and been rewarded with impressive results proportionate to their daring. To me their art seems heroic in the way of which I wrote earlier in these pages: the imaginative extension of experience. Parallel with their intensification of imagery, there has been in

78

process a strong current toward the non-figurative (usually but rather inaccurately called abstraction) which has already attained one climax—its romantic one—in action-painting (usually but rather inaccurately called abstract expressionism). I feel the same kind of admiration for some of these adventurers that I feel for the courage of the other two, but the pictorial consequences of their ideas about painting present several difficulties for me.

Hans Hofmann has now for some years been both the teaching father of the younger action-painters and one of the best-known practitioners of the style. In age he is two generations older than those of his followers who are in their twenties; in boldness of execution they can hardly match him. With good luck, what is recklessness in youth becomes assurance in age. His painting at Nebraska, interesting in its own right, is not typical of action-painting as I propose to define it for this discussion. In *The Fruit Bowl* (page 81) there is still a connection with nature in the recognizability of the shapes, even though that connection is so tenuous that the outlines are almost at the point of becoming a diagram. The objects and their setting are simply an occasion for composing a series of interlocking directional lines which go far toward the non-figuration which prevails in fully developed action-painting. The pictorial character of the design is contained energy, but the emphasis is so strongly linear that the pigment is little more than a stain. Thus the picture lacks the second major trait of action-painting, which is a dramatization of the pigment not only by the stroke of the brush but also by the flourish and often the thickness of the impasto. In these two prime features of the "school" practice, other paintings by Hofmann himself are exemplary.

There is one other difference between *The Fruit Bowl* and Hofmann's own action-paintings that is peculiar to him. Its thinly painted schematized drawing, lightly lyrical in activity, leads the eye about the picture from point to point, so that the full apprehension of it requires a perceptible though very brief interval of time. Hofmann's more active pictures, in which the ridges and valleys of pigment engage in a coloristic struggle which he himself has described by the relatively mild phrase of "push-and-pull", make everything happen both explosively and simultaneously. I know of no other painter except Marin whose pictures habitually overcome the usual successive effect of many strokes by merging them into a single unified impact upon the eye.

For the essential action-painting characteristics of nonfiguration and a complete reliance upon gesture with the brush, Theodoros Stamos's *A Walk in the Poppies* (page 85) is satisfactorily typical of the school. The activity in this painting is abstract in respect to imagery and is momentary in respect to content. It is made out of what happens within the painter during the time of painting. But for what I want to say about action-painting as the present romantic climax of the now long-continued tendency to minimize and eliminate imagery, I should like it to be understood that I have in mind not only the "school" works of Hofmann but also pictures by Franz Kline, Willem de Kooning, and the school's dead hero, Jackson Pollock.

An action-painting is the autobiography of the mo-

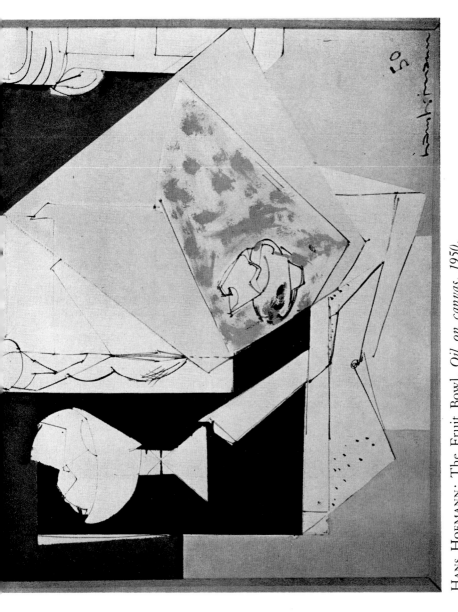

HANS HOFMANN: The Fruit Bowl. *Oil on canvas, 1950,* 29⅞″ x 38″. Collection of the Nebraska Art Association, University of Nebraska Art Galleries.

ment. The painter paints the state of his mind during the
time of painting, if I correctly understand the intention;
of course, that state of mind is in a sense the sum total
of what has happened to him up to that time, but ideally
nothing occurs in the painting that is not immediate and
spontaneous. The picture is an improvisation parallel to
that of the pianist, with all that this implies as to the im-
mense amount of practice necessary for successful improvisation, the knowledge of the resources of the medium, the special kind of skill in execution. Communication here is not by means of representation or symbols,
but through color and handling. This gesturing in paint
makes an object (the picture) which is wordless, sound-
less, and without motion; but it is full of color clashes and
harmonies, strokes that shout or whisper, full of move-
ment in the pigment itself and of space sensations in the
shifting of colors backward and forward all over the
canvas. The painting is itself the act of living at the time
the painting is done. It is the graph of a dance in life,
and catches the life through the unique characteristic of
pigment—its responsiveness to the gesturing arm and
hand.

Action-painting seems to many people entirely un-
natural, whereas it is only extremely unnaturalistic. It
does not correspond to the optical observation of nature.
But action-painting is entirely natural in the painting of
the twentieth century because it is suited to the nature of
pigment. It is also highly artificial because success with
it requires a high degree of artifice. In both respects it
seems to me to have had a literary precursor in the poetry
of Gerard Manley Hopkins. The literary critic William

York Tindall has pointed out how a poem by Hopkins is not a recollection in tranquillity but experience in process. That is a deeper correspondence with action-painting than what I am noting here; this is that the artifice of Hopkins's handling of words was a natural development in accordance with the nature of the English language. After that came the more daring but quite logical experiments of James Joyce and Gertrude Stein.

My personal difficulties with action-painting do not, I think, include unresponsiveness to the pictures so long as I am in their presence. But I find myself unable so far to take away with me enough to be sure than anything permanent has happened to me. The experience of art, like all other kinds of experience, takes on meaning for me in proportion to my ability to think about it; and for thinking about a painting I must be able to recall the picture with a fair degree of faithfulness. The free-swinging procedures of the action-painters and the visually amorphous character of their results makes it impossible for my memory to retain the individual picture precisely enough to permit the imaginative re-experience which I ask of art.

This seems to me a serious drawback, for the action-painter intends to communicate something—himself. Since his effort is not as effective with me as I should like it to be, I am inclined to wonder whether the action-painter's way of insisting upon himself is a closer approach to reality or a flight from it. The answer is, I suggest provisionally, that it is both. The calligraphy of his immediate feelings is validly real for him because it is himself at the moment; and when he is done he exists there

THEODOROS STAMOS: A Walk in the Poppies. *Oil on canvas,*
55″ x 40″.

on the canvas for himself, at least. One action-painter has indeed described the act of painting as "a desperate bid for individuality". I do not attach much general significance to what may be in me the private defect of a poorly functioning memory; but my inability to achieve a satisfying coherent idea of the painting-personalities of Pollock and de Kooning and the later Hofmann may indicate something.

The total reality of art must include an audience, and the audience must be renewed down the generations if the art is to become part of a culture. The self-subsisting character of the universe is not repeated by art. The cosmos will lose no inherent reality even if man, by destroying himself, is no longer here to be aware of it. But art has no such independent life; the material survival of St. Peter's cathedral or Pollock's *Autumn Rhythm* (Metropolitan Museum of Art, New York) will have meaning, will possess full reality, only so long as men and women stay around and value the experience it gives them. The work of art gives out life by receiving it.

But after all and on the other hand, there is no compelling reason, either moral or esthetic, why every picture, or any picture, should be permanently effective or should last forever. The ephemeral is as appropriate in art as this age thinks it is in other possessions. In a civilization whose dynamics seem to require that things be replaced even before they are worn out, temporariness in paintings may be an appropriate virtue. To be sure, human nature is much older than this century; and even the most venturesome artist may have difficulty in adjusting to the fate of being contemporaneous only. As a member of the audi-

ence I think it quite sufficient if a contemporary picture
gives me a momentary freshness; even if I can't retain
it for renewed satisfaction, I have still had it once. So
I shall not be either surprised or chagrined if action-painting proves to be almost as evanescent as art criticism itself.

XIV

Coloristic Purism

MARK ROTHKO
(1903-)

THOUGH MARK ROTHKO IS often called an action-painter, he does not seem one to me; but there is as yet no generally accepted label with which to differentiate him. From some of his experiments in what I call coloristic purism I take away something lasting, something to think about; and one reason is that he seems considerably less insistent upon making me think while I am looking at his pictures. For instance, *Orange and Yellow* (Albright Art Gallery, Buffalo) (opposite page 90), in all its seven-foot-seven-inch hugeness, makes no overt comment on life, does not even imply any involvement with life that I can see beyond affirming a consuming intensity of color sensation. It displays nothing of the often frenetic activity of action-painting; it might be thought that the painter had succeeded in suppressing himself and substituting the impersonal radiation of a particular kind of matter as the picture's only reason for existence. This apparent impersonality is eminently a classic intention, but color is itself inherently romantic. Thus Rothko's kind of painting is what I interpret as the romantically classic climax to the theory of the self-sufficing reality of pigment. Classic purity and romantic intensity co-exist in a tense equilibrium. Or rather: abstract statement (non-figuration) and sensuous reality (pigment) have become one thing.

Once painting crossed the divide with Prendergast, an ultimate like this became not only possible but also, in the artistic climate of the twentieth century, quite logical. It is the consequence of a fact once put into words by Gauguin: ". . . color which, like music, is vibration, achieves what is vaguest and most universal in nature— her inmost force." My experience is that before a successful picture by Rothko the first thing to understand is that it is not necessary to understand the experience at the time of having it. The intellect need not be busy for the duration of the sensation. Understanding, to whatever degree one needs it, can come later. This is the first and the last reality of paint. The pulsation of color surrounds me, envelops me, penetrates me, saturates me. In this projective force the painter seems to have become invisible, and the picture's seeming reticence about him only increases its power over the sensibility of another. Where de Kooning and Hofmann startle me with a conflagration, the impasto and tactility of a Rothko light a slow burn which prolongs itself in my consciousness as no example of brush gesticulation has yet done.

MARK ROTHKO: Orange and Yellow. *Oil on canvas, 1956,* 91″ x 71″. Courtesy of the Albright Art Gallery, gift of Mr. Seymour H. Knox.

For a further indication of what I experience with a Rothko painting I draw upon the Czech writer, Karel Capek:

> . . . To be like a stone, but without weight. To be like water, but without reflection. To be like a cloud, but without movement. To be like an animal, but without hunger. To be like a man, but without thoughts. . . .

That kind of experience seems important to me because it is on that level of primal response that true personality begins. The life of thought is worth little unless thinking remains continually aware of its sources. And so far as I can make out, color produces the first individualized response of the whole human creature to visual experience. A successful painting by Rothko is one manifestation of the final mysticism of matter—as mysterious and as miraculous as any fancied immateriality. Before a Rothko painting the pronouncing word is not the secondary thing: to do. The pronouncing word is: to be.

XV

Postscript

TWO OF THE CONTEMPORARY ultimates have together been the goal of this discussion; they must also be the end of it even though it leaves the presentation of how things are at the moment very incomplete. To attempt an adequate panorama would require a still longer title: From Realism to Reality—and Beyond. All I have attempted here is to thread out one line of development in American painting as I have experienced it. Pigmental reality as an ideal has resulted in several variants of intense purity; in many pictures so motivated the intentional asceticism in imagery has given a compensating intensity of sensation.

But the purity of those pictures does not, to my way of thinking, make their makers into pure painters. For this kind of purity is achieved by exclusion, and the decisions as to what to exclude derive from intellectual theorizings about what painting ought to be. It is not thinking that constricts painting, but thinking in certain ways; thinking about how much can be included in painting won't harm any painter who is so purely a painter that he can paint anything without compromising his paint. The purer the painter, the safer he is from being corrupted by pictorial content. What may theoretically be the visual corruption of the recognizable may also be, without impairing the reality inherent in paint, the means of adding a new realism to the total reality that is feasible in the pictorial experience.

I have been temperamentally lucky in that the painters who interest me most were and still are the experimenters, whose works I have found to be often as strange and as exciting as life itself. But I make a distinction between this interest, this curiosity about the new as being possibly a significant change in man, and the renewable pleasure from pictures that renew themselves and me. Because these are an essential part of what makes me glad to have been born, I value them most. Because I have lived as long as I have, I look upon the current experiments in paint as only the latest word, not the last. But the experimental pictures now current are nevertheless an important part of what makes me glad to be still alive.

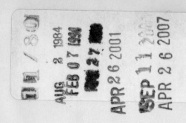